Your Dreams of Sex, Love and Romance and What They Mean

Laura Suzanne

This book is dedicated to Tiger Snell, my faithful companion who was by my side the entire time I was writing this book.

Acknowledgements:

I would like to give thanks to my friends and family for their support throughout this journey. Special thanks to Roy Snell, Victoria Gallagher, Janis Abriel, Leeza Robertson, Stacey Chester, Ellen Greenlee, Juanita Curiel, Helen Baucum, Patrick Curry, Gypsy, Barbara Buchanan, Amy Barilla, Janice Masters, Kim O'Neil, Christine Briscoe, Jennifer Huse, Sara Bruestle, Sharon Savage and, most of all, Mom.

Forward

There is a fantastic place in your mind which you experience each time you fall asleep. A summit within the deepest part of your mind, where extraordinary thoughts happen, where you can give or receive messages through your subconscious mind. Your mind records and remembers every experience you have ever had, including all of your dreams. It stores this information in your subconscious mind. But just how do you make use of that information?

That is exactly what my colleague and friend, Laura Suzanne Snell will help you do as she takes you on an important journey of self-discovery and a deeper understanding of your dreams and what they mean in her new book, "*Your Dreams of Sex, Love and Romance and What They Mean*".

Every time you fall asleep, you dream. Your dream time is like an untold story, the true story underneath the surface, about what's really happening in your life.

By reading this engaging book, you will soon realize that YOU ARE a dream interpreter and this book will help you decipher the hidden meaning contained within the dreams.

All of your dreams are thoughts from your own unconscious mind, so of course, it stands to reason that they are somehow connected to who you are and your own reality. Some dreams make sense to you right away, you get them, and know why you had them. It's those dreams that do not make sense right away, that leave you puzzled, that have a deeper meaning which you are about to find out in "Your Dreams of Sex, Love and Romance and What They Mean".

Having been in the personal growth industry since the late 90's, I first came to know Laura through the dream interpretation column she wrote for the Las Vegas Weekly. Impressed with her deep intuition and abilities, I felt she would make a tremendous impact as a guest on the radio show I hosted, "Hyptalk."

As it turned out, Laura brought such a special charm, insight and wisdom to the show that I later asked her to be my co-host.

Laura has always had wonderful intuition and skill and so it's no surprise she decided to utilize her special gift and pass along this incredible wisdom to you as a way to help you gain self-awareness and clarity through recalling and interpreting your own dreams.

While, there are other books on the market that provide basic dream meanings, this book not only provides some of the most common dream definitions, but it goes well beyond that.

The truth is, as you'll quickly realize in "Your Dreams of Sex, Love and Romance and What They Mean", your dreams have their own significant, unique and personal meaning to you.

You will gain more than knowledge. You will gain the wisdom of how to decode the secret language of your subconscious mind and your dreams will now take on a whole new dimension and become more of a learning tool for you.

I can tell you as a Certified Clinical Hypnotherapist since 1999, there is much more to you that you are fully aware of. Gaining awareness of who you really are however, is one of the great benefits worth exploring as you delve into this fascinating area of your mind through the insights presented to you in your dreams.

As you read this book, you will come to a place, as I did, which creates a feeling of confidence that you really are capable of interpreting your own dreams.

Laura provides ample examples and tools to help you do just that. With a little time, practice and patience, you'll be looking at the signs revealed to you within your dreams and gaining a deeper understanding about yourself as a result.

As you progress and get better at interpreting your dreams, it will simply become more natural for you to ask yourself the proper questions, instantaneously, such as the questions Laura suggests in "Your Dreams of Sex, Love and Romance and What They Mean"and to be able to quickly draw your own conclusions from your internal resources within and from your life experience to help guide you to know what your dreams are about the moment you do remember them.

With Laura's gift of being empathic, I couldn't be happier that she has decided put all her insights down in this wonderful book to assist you in your journey and I know it will help you grow in love, health, and wealth.

--Victoria Gallagher
http://www.hyptalk.com

Introduction

This book is your guide to understanding your dreams and deciphering what they mean. This book was originally a compilation of newspaper columns featuring dreams submitted to me by my readers and my interpretation of their dreams. Being that were well over one hundred dreams in the collection, I chose to make this into three separate books broken down by category. This book, the first in a three-part series, is all about your dreams of sex, love and romance interpreted. I have used real-life dreams from actual readers to illustrate my points and my interpretations of these dreams. There will also be exercises for you, the reader, to give personal meaning to your dreams and decode the messages from your subconscious mind.

In Chapter One, we will discuss the importance of dreams; why you have them and how you can begin to connect with and understand them better. Chapter Two is where we explore sexual dreams, common scenarios, their symbolism and meaning. Chapter Three is about real dreams of love and romance from my personal journal and those of my readers, and my interpretations of them. Chapter Four focuses on relationship issues and how to use your dreams to spot potential problems in relationships early on. Chapter Five is about examining your own role in relationships and using your dreams as a yardstick to measure results, thereby determining if you are on track and if you are liking what you are creating for yourself. Chapter Six is where we delve into dreams of fantasy and desire, expression and repression, and what secrets they reveal. Chapter Seven is a brief introduction to the art of the dream journal. Chapter Eight covers the prelude to having a great night of romantic dreaming and, lastly, Chapter Nine walks you through a simple step-by-step method on how to break down and interpret your own dreams.

Chapter One: The Importance of Your Dreams and Why You Have Them

Everyone dreams. We do not always remember what we dream about, however, we all have dreams when we are asleep. Some dreams are in color while some are in black in white. Some will seem obvious or be very vivid, while others are vague and elusive, almost uneventful. A dream can often look like a nonsensical mishmash of images strewn together that resemble pieces of a puzzle that will never be solved. To have a dream can simply be a brain dump; a subconscious regurgitation of the previous day's events as a method of cleaning house. They can play out like a movie, sometimes scary, sometimes comical, sometimes erotic. At times it can be frustrating and confusing trying to make sense of them, but the more that you make a conscious effort to connect with them, the easier it gets to truly know their meaning.

To have a dream is tantamount to getting a letter from a trusted friend. You would not even consider just throwing it away unopened, would you? I didn't think so! That is what you are doing when you do not pay much attention or just flat out ignore your dream. It is like deleting an email, status unread, when within the body of the letter contains a precious gift – a message from your higher self delivered via your subconscious mind, expressly for you. The fact that you are reading this book suggests that you have a desire to be more in tune with and to learn from your nightly excursions.

The key to understanding your dreams is to first pay attention and look for the obvious. What stands out? Who were the key players; people, animals, etc. in the dream? What was your role? What was the setting; outdoors, building, vehicle, etc.? What was the time frame: past, present or future? What was the emotional climate, feeling or sensation in the dream? Try to recall anything and everything that you can remember about the dream, no matter how small or insignificant it may seem at the time. If it was there, and you were aware of it – a lipstick stain on a glass, for example – it is a significant part of the dream and not to be overlooked. You may not understand it now, but by the time you are finished reading this book, you will have far greater insight into your own dreams.

Your dream is always telling you something about yourself and what is going on in your life, sometimes it will be very simple and obvious, and often times it will appear a bit more cryptic. I have seen which lovers I can trust and which ones will disappoint me in a dream. I have been given clues about the intentions of potential suitors, and had future premonitions about them all while dreaming. I always take the time to listen to what my dream has to say and how I can apply it to my daily life.

Some dreams will have more meaning to you than others and will make more of an impact. Some are very basic but they always have a meaning no matter how trivial they seem at first. If you dream of roses, for example, that could mean that you are about to "blossom" or "come into bloom" in your personal or professional life. Perhaps you will meet your soulmate or get that big promotion? There are so many symbols, and each is subject to your own personal interpretation. Yes, you can certainly look at definitions in a dream book, and there are several good ones available. I have my own version available online that you are welcome to look at, as well. However, instead of relying on someone else to tell you what your dream means, it is always better to go directly to the source and ask the right question: "What does this dream mean to ME?"

It really is a personal journey unique to the dreamer to decode a dream, as the meaning can vary greatly from one individual to another. To see a red rose, for example, would generally be seen as a precursor to romance. Roses are beautiful and they sure do smell great! The color of the rose will have a different meaning, too. Is it red (romance) yellow (friendship) or black (death)? Perhaps to see a rose is your higher self telling you to stop and take a minute to "smell the roses," to be more present and enjoy life more. However, if you work tending a rose garden or in a flower shop, there more be a more mundane aspect to your dream.

With all of the many dreams that were submitted to me via email and in person for interpretation from clients, my job was not to provide them with a canned definition, but to help them extract the meaning specific to them. A person who works as a gardener would have a very different take on roses than would a beauty pageant contestant to whom roses are presented as a prize. One might view it as their daily grind, where the other may see it as a reward. What is your definition of a rose? Love them or hate them? Favorite color of rose and why? This will help you to personalize it as it pertains to you. I am here to guide you, however, you are always your own best authority on everything, dream interpretation included.

Chapter Two: Sexual Dreams: Popular Symbolism and Meaning

Sex. Such a small word with such a big meaning, and for many a taboo topic. Depending on where you are from and how you were raised, it can be a source of pleasure or shame. Sex dreams are sometimes reflections of desire, sometimes they are simply just a way to relieve sexual tension. Nocturnal emissions or "wet dreams" are a physical release that happen while sleeping, the physiological response to a sexual dream. In a lot of cases, the dreamer does not even remember what the dream was about, but there is evidence to prove it. They had a sexually-charged dream which caused them to be aroused and ejaculate while sleeping. Boys going through puberty are often embarrassed by this; for women it is a little less obvious. Having a sensual dream can be very pleasant, indeed, and I think a lot of women who have read "Fifty Shades of Grey" found themselves waking up with smiles to rival the Cheshire Cat due to the clandestine nature of the book.

What are some of the universal symbols that might appear in sexual dreams? The act of sex itself can be symbolic of integration and unity. The black and the white can represent opposition and duality, the yin (feminine) and the yang (masculine) are common symbols found in dreams about sex. Phallic symbols, such as bananas, swords or cigars, may be images relating to the male genitals, whereas flowers or a garden (Adam and Eve) or fruit – a succulent, juicy peach – or an apple (forbidden fruit) may represent the female private parts. A horse or "stallion," sometimes a canine (men are often referred to as dogs) may depict male sexual energy, whereas a sleek jungle cat, "cougar" or "panther" may embody the female essence. This is just a small sample of what may pop up (no pun intended) in your sex dreams.

To have sex with someone is to take on an aspect of that person and to give something of yourself. There are definitely some "strange bedfellows" in our dreams. We may dream of having sex with our dead grandmother, priest or even a random stranger. These dreams have the only the meaning that we give to them, and by using your own personal definitions you will soon realize that you are not a pervert for dreaming of sex with someone that you and society deem inappropriate. It is probably somewhere along the lines of wanting something that this person has, be it a personal quality like confidence or poise, status and power, or even a possession. Something that you wish to acquire or develop further within yourself is usually the meaning behind dreaming of having sex with someone ideal or adverse. (We will delve deeper into this in Chapter Six: Dreams of Fantasy and Desire.)

To dream of being intimate with a same-sex partner does not mean that you are gay if you are not, just like a dream of having sex with a relative does not suggest that you are a sexual deviant or mentally disturbed, if you are not. If you do have such a dream, it may simply mean that your masculine and feminine energies are out of sync and this "union" is helping to balance those aspects. If you are homosexual or bisexual, then the meaning may be slightly different, depending on who the subject is. If it is your brother or grandmother, I would venture to say that it has a similar meaning as it would for someone who is heterosexual, as most people, gay or straight, do not generally desire their brother or grandmother in an incestuous way. Once again, it is always up to the dreamer to define the nature of each relationship and determine the true meaning.

Here is an example of such a dream from one of my readers, followed by my take on it: I would say that the meaning would be very similar regardless of the sexual orientation of the dreamer. In this particular case, the person who submitted the dream was male, dreaming of a woman.

Dear Laura,

I recently dreamed about a woman I met several months ago at a conference. Despite the fact that we live in different cities, we have since kept in touch and I feel increasingly drawn to her. In the dream, we are little and munchkins dressed in old fashioned nightgowns. We are jumping up and down on my bed, giggling like little children.

–Confused Munchkin

Dear Munchkin,

What a cute dream! This is definitely a message from your "inner child" to lighten up and to get out and play more. The woman mirrors the child inside of you, thus you are drawn to her feminine, playful energy. She may also have the qualities that you admire and would like to cultivate into your own persona, so you will want to identify what those are. Nightgowns and the bed suggest a need for rest and relaxation or some "down time." Your dream is telling you that you are stressed and taking yourself and life much too seriously. Fairies, elves and goblins are our spiritual helpers. All work and no play makes Jack a dull boy, so get out and have some fun, Munchkin!

Note: The only thing I would say might be different, is if the dream had been about two men or two women, it would balance the aspects of the male/female energy, as we each have elements of both within us. Balancing these energies within ourselves is something that we all experience, regardless of our sexual preference. Had the dreamer been bisexual, the same concept would apply.

Chapter Three: Real Dreams of Love and Romance Interpreted

The first dream I will interpret was taken directly from my dream journal. I am honored to share it with you, as it was very profound and close to my heart. The second is from one of my readers. I gave each of them a title, a date, a category and listed who was featured in the dream. I find this helpful in remembering dreams, as I can reference them quickly when I want to look back at them later. This is a very good habit to get into when recording your dreams.

Title: Anima/Animus
Category: Self-love/Romance
Starring: Myself as both male and female

This was probably the single best dream I have had so far! I can still remember it like it was yesterday. I was making copies at Kinko's copy center and, from across the room, I saw the most gorgeous man I have ever laid eyes on. He stood about 6 feet tall, lean yet muscular, dressed in faded jeans and a purple shirt. He brushed a lock of strawberry blond hair from his brow, exposing flawless skin and brilliant blue eyes. His features were chiseled, his smile dazzling white… I was enthralled. The energy he emitted was masculine, containing aspects of the feminine as well, making for a synergistic blend of the yin and yang. I felt a magnetic pull that was stronger than anything I had ever experienced!

I was drawn into him, and it was as if we were one being. The emotions that I felt went something like this: jubilation, lust, ecstasy, wonderment, unity. I never imagined that I could feel such a strong degree of love, attraction and desire for another person, and I was a happily married woman at the time! However, this "dream man" was not actually another person… as I separated from him and stood back, I noticed that he bore and uncanny resemblance to ME! "He looks like the male version of me," I recall thinking when I saw him up close. His beautiful energy felt so closely matched to my own that I realized this man IS me! He is my male counterpart, my "animus," as the Jungians would call him. That explained that feeling of perfect love that I had yet to experience with a flesh-and-blood man. This man that I was loving so much was a part of my own being, and the attraction was one that I could not resist. I was completely captivated by my inner male. Coming from a lineage of dominant women, I repressed that within myself, as I did not feel that is what a woman should be. I found aggressive male energy oppressive and distasteful, and purposely attracted a rather passive man for a marriage partner, who battled with his own inner male and female. We are always seeking balance, and sometimes it takes a lifetime to achieve that.

This dream was very soothing to my soul, as I was able to feel the beauty, grace and power of my male side and to rejoice in it. I did not have to be afraid of it or try to disconnect from it any longer. Any negative associations I may have had were replaced by knowing what it was like to experience a perfectly blended union of the male/female energy. For so long I had searched for "true love" with a partner, not realizing that what we seek exists within us. I found my "dream man" in my inner male every bit as wonderful as I knew he would be. I visit the dream world whenever I feel the need to connect with him, yet I know that he is within me and I am within him. We are truly two aspects of the same being. It goes without saying that I make a really handsome man! The purple shirt that he wore represents the crown chakra, the highest part of ourselves and our connection to the source. I believe that I was at Kinko's copy center because I wished to make an imprint, as I was working on these issues and doing a lot of teaching and consulting at the time. To me, a copy machine meant that I wanted to get my message out to as many people as possible. This is an experience I would be happy to duplicate!

The next dream was submitted by Damon, a young man who was one of my readers.

Dear Laura:

I had a dream that I asked you out on a date and you said yes. I came to your door in a tux, with a dozen red roses and we got into the car, but it turned into a horse and carriage. The roses turned into different types of flowers and changed sizes. We got into the carriage and rode off, and all I could see was a sunset.

–Damon

Dear Damon,

That certainly sounds like a dream date to me! The fact that you are wearing a tuxedo in the dream shows that you are wanting to put your best foot forward, and may also have a tendency to see things as black or white, given that a tux is usually black and white. This can also represent the yin and the yang, the dark and the light, etc. There is a symbiotic blend of male/female energy, as both man and woman are riding together in your chosen vehicle for growth. At first it was a car, a vehicle which allows you to move at high speeds, then it changed to a carriage, a vehicle that allows you to move more slowly and enjoy the sights along the way. There was a horse, a very powerful masculine animal that we rely on for transportation or working in the fields. He was pulling the carriage. This indicates that you are feeling very comfortable letting your male side take the lead in the dream and in life.

The flowers represent your spiritual self coming into full bloom. First, you selected roses, which are popular and traditional for a romantic gesture. Red is a power color, symbolizing the root chakra (survival, procreation, tribal) as well as lust and passion. A dozen roses is 12 broken down is one plus two equals three. The number three symbolizes the trinity. You may want to consult a numerology book to see if there is anything relating to the numbers 12 and three that pertains to you. Numbers are significant in dreams, and sometimes they will resurface. I know a woman who saw a phone number in a dream and it turned out to belong to her sister that she had been trying to reach! Pay attention to numbers!

As the dream progressed, the flowers changed from roses into garden-variety flowers. I am thinking that while you

23

are a traditional man in some ways, you are also someone who likes to be daring and adventurous, do things your way, and believe that variety is the spice of life. Noticing the sunset and riding off into it with someone special is featured in this dream. A sunset is a beautiful sight and would set the state for romance. It also symbolizes the end of the work day, or the "happily ever after" aspect of life. You said that "all you could see was a sunset." You are looking forward to the end of your single days and to being part of a couple. Best of luck to you in finding her, Damon. According to your dream, you are ready for love!

Those are two dreams from real people, myself and Damon, from the year 2000 that I have shared with you, followed by my interpretation of each. If these were your dreams, what would your interpretations be? I hope that I have planted the seed and you are starting to think about that as we continue forward on this journey.

Chapter Four: Relationship Red Flags: How to Spot them in Dreams

I receive a lot of information about my relationships through my dreams, some of it good, some of it not so good. As hard as it is to face the unpleasant part, I realize that the dream is a message from my higher consciousness telling me that something is not right. An example of this is that, for many years, I would dream that that my husband left me for another woman. I recall having that dream frequently, and it was always the same: I would always have this dream early on a Sunday morning, and wake up with that sinking feeling that our marriage was not going to last forever. I would tell him about it, and each time he would tell me that it was just my fear of abandonment rearing its ugly head and to brush it off. My spirit was preparing me for what was to come, and even though I did not want to believe it, there was a part of me that knew it was true. I started having this dream about two years into our marriage, and we finally divorced after nearly 10 years of being married. My husband started seeing another woman while we were still married, just as my dream indicated that he would do. She was not the cause of our divorce, however, she was the justification.

Unfortunately, I was already two years into my marriage when this dream sequence started, so it was too late to heed the warning signals and do anything but wait and prepare myself for the inevitable. I am now divorced and dating, so I am hyperaware of what my dreams are showing me about each man that comes my way. I would like to share some examples with you of red flags that have come through in my dreams with the hopes that you will be able to take this information and learn from it.

Let's start with Christopher: I was briefly engaged to him in my 20s, and it was a long-distance relationship. I was going to relocate to the East Coast to be with him and probably have to give my dog up in the process. Thank God I had dreams that showed me who he really was or I would have made a huge mistake and uprooted myself for nothing.

On the surface he appeared stable: He had a new car, lived in a nice condo and had been with the same company for many years. He was very family-oriented and a gentleman. He seemed like a great catch. Because we lived on opposite coasts, and did not see each other on a daily basis, it was very easy for him to hide the fact that he had a drug and gambling problem. As intuitive as I was and am, he was the master of deception, so I did not see the red flags right away. The inconsistencies started showing up in my dreams toward the end of the relationship, and then I began to see what was really going on.

There was one dream where I was sitting in the backseat of a car and he was driving. He had grown a beard, which covered a lot of his face. This was odd to me, as I had only ever seen him clean shaven. He was also wearing dark sunglasses, which were not his usual style. He would not turn around and look at me or even acknowledge that I was present when I attempted to speak to him. In yet another dream, I went to his house and no one was home. The house was empty! Both the interior and exterior were a pale shade of yellow. This was not the same place he had taken me to when I had been to visit him, however, the dream was showing me that this was the place he called home.

It may seem obvious to anyone reading this that he was not ready to get married. It would have been obvious to me had we not rushed into an engagement after a whirlwind courtship and spent very little face-to-face time together. The whole relationship spanned about four months, and while there were visits back and forth, it was mostly telephone and email communication. My dream revealed that he was not emotionally available and certainly not focused on the relationship, as he was driving and I was sitting alone in the backseat… or "taking a backseat" to his addictions. He was hiding behind a beard and sunglasses because there were things that he definitely did not want me to see, hence the need to "cover up." He had his back to me and would not look at or talk to me for the duration of the dream. Toward the end of the relationship, I could feel that he had "tuned me out," as the communication just was not there.

The pale yellow, empty house can mean different things. In this case, the house represents the state of consciousness of the person in question. The fact that the house was empty confirmed that he was not present in our relationship and used substances to disconnect. The lights were on, but no one was home. The pale yellow color showed me that his solar plexus, or center of the will and self-esteem, was very weak, hence the lighter color. This was a person who was struggling to keep up the façade that all was well when, in fact, it was not. He had a good job and people who depended on him, so he was trying to keep it together so that no one was the wiser. Yellow has also been used to describe someone who is a coward: "Yellow-bellied coward." In a sense, that would be accurate for my former fiancé, as he was dishonest about who he was and his intentions. He was keeping secrets from me and lying to everyone, most of all to himself. He did not even have the courage to break off the engagement with integrity. He just became more and more distant and, when I asked him what was going on, he told me that he could not do this anymore and did not give me much of an explanation. My dream showed me that he was turning his back to me and ignoring me, which is basically what happened.

I am fortunate that my subconscious mind was there to save me from making a huge mistake. The signs were there, and my dream spelled out for me all of the things that I was not ready or able to see in my waking state. There have been similar dreams about other men I have dated that give clues about them, their agendas and the nature of our relationship. There was a dream I had recently about Jeff, a man I was seeing. In the dream, we had just been intimate. Immediately afterward, he was looking at himself in the mirror naked, critiquing his body, and seemed completely oblivious to the fact that I was still in his bed. He got word about an indie film looking for actors, so off he went to investigate, without even acknowledging me! He just left me there in his bed, alone, and went on his merry way! If that is not a definitive sign that this man was self-absorbed and just using me, I don't know what is. There were other dreams along the same vein that showed his intentions toward me were less than noble and that there was an emotionally unstable aspect to him. The bottom line is that it was "all about him." This man was completely self-absorbed and did not care about me at all! I stopped seeing him soon after, as I was noticing that the behavior witnessed in my waking life was consistent with what played out in the dream world. We were just not on the same page as far as what we wanted in a relationship, nor was he capable of giving me what I needed, so I was quick to move on and my dreams just made it easier to do so.

There was yet another man, Jerry, I dated last year who was newly divorced. I had reservations going in about his ability to be in another relationship so soon, and wondered if he had truly recovered from his marriage ending, as it had been a long one. I was very taken with him and he with me, so I gave him the benefit of the doubt. Soon after we started dating, I had a dream that we were at a picnic hosted by his family and friends. I was standing behind him holding a plate of food, waiting for him to move over so I would have a place to sit beside him at the picnic table. There was very little room at the table, and he was sitting closer to the end. As I stood there waiting, he simply continued eating and talking, never once looking in my direction or making a place for me to join him. Hmmm. That dream was very telling. I could most definitely see the parallels between the waking and the sleeping worlds. He was very hot and cold, giving me mixed messages about the level of involvement he wanted from me in real life, and this dream really magnified that. I broke it off with him soon after having this nocturnal experience, as I could see this was yet another man who was clearly not ready for a relationship with me.

I am thankful that these dreams were there to give me the clarity and the confirmation that I needed, and always in the nick of time. My dreams will let me know in no uncertain terms if a relationship is going to be good for me or not. I will always heed them, too, as they are very powerful. I hope that you can glean something from this chapter, and look for the signs in your own dreams about your relationships or potential suitors, as they are designed to show you what you may not yet be aware of in your waking life. It is important to be the objective observer: Look at the scenarios being played out in your dreams and be a good witness. What is happening in the dream? What is his or her role? What is your role? What is the overarching feeling in the dream and upon waking? Is it different?

Think of it like you are watching a TV show or movie, and you can press pause, or hit rewind and go back later to review it if need be. How does what you saw in the dream compare to what is happening in your relationship now? If you liked what you saw and feel that you are in a good relationship, this is cause for celebration, as your conscious and subconscious are in alignment. However, if this was something that you did not want to see, make sure that it is valid before ending the relationship. If you dream that your partner is cheating on you, for example, that may be the case … or it may just be your fears coming up and needing to be addressed. I would advise you to use the information for what it is, a tool to dig deeper and discover the truth about yourself and your relationship before taking any action.

Chapter Five: Looking For Love: How Your Dreams Can Help You Find It

In the last chapter, we talked about being open to the warning signs that your dreams give you to tell you that something is amiss with your relationship or potential relationship. In this chapter, we are going to do the opposite. We are going to use the dream sequences to see what we are creating in our quest for love and to ask ourselves if this is what we truly want. We are all the actor, director and producer in our own dream movie. If we do not like it, we have the ability to change it.

The question is, what are you looking for? "Love… everyone wants it, not everyone finds it" is a direct quote from Patti Stanger, the "Millionaire Matchmaker" from the hit series on Bravo. This is true, we seek love and often give into instant gratification while going against our better judgment in choosing a partner. Remember the Johnny Lee song "Looking for Love In All The Wrong Places" from the movie "Urban Cowboy"? The lyrics begin with "I've spent a lifetime looking for you, singles bars and good time lovers never true." I think it is safe to say that we have all been there and done that, settled for quantity or convenience when what we seek is quality. While it may have worked out for Bud and Sissy in the movie, the reality is that marrying someone you barely know, like they did, is not advisable.

I cannot tell you where or how to find your perfect partner, or what your criteria should be, however, I can tell you that it is very important to be crystal clear on what you want from a relationship before you take that first step. So when you are looking for love, what exactly are you looking for? Making a list of what you want in a partner and how you would like your relationship to be is of vital importance. For example, "I am looking for someone who is financially and emotionally stable, has good character and a great sense of humor. Someone who likes to travel and who is an animal lover. I would like to have a relationship where we are open to growth and bring out the best in one another."

There are three pertinent questions that I ask myself regarding each potential partner.

1.	Is this person ready to be in a relationship with me, and do we share similar values?

2.	Can I bring this person around my friends and family without feeling like I have to make excuses for or be embarrassed by them?

3.	Would this person be acceptable for my mother, sister or best friend to date?

This is some serious food for thought when it comes to setting your intentions and creating the space for your relationship to manifest. Here is how your dreaming mind can help to do just that.

Your dream self will be your oracle, best friend and GPS are rolled into one. This is good stuff! It will cost you nothing, and you do not have to consult a psychic or ask your friends for the umpteenth time if they think this person is right for you. All you have to do is open your very own dream journal, and the clues will be right there. Match what you see within your dreams to what you are feeling, and you will know if you are on the right track or not. Your feelings do not lie… that still small voice may speak to you in a whisper… or sometimes a scream. Your dreams will show you scenarios that your waking mind cannot. There is a widely held belief that to be in the dream state is to walk through the portal to the other dimensions and realities, bypassing the critical conscious mind, where you are able to receive information that you would not be privy to otherwise.

Here are two dreams from my readers that beautifully illustrate my point. The first one is the sign of an iffy relationship, the second shows that the dreamer is on track to getting what she wants in her relationship.

Dear Laura,

I dreamed that I was at a big arts and crafts fair. My boyfriend had a booth and was painting pictures of people. I asked him to paint one, and he said he would. I wandered off to see what else they had at this fair. Everyone I encountered was someone from my past who had wronged me in some way. I could not believe that all these people were gathered in one place at one time. I walked back to my boyfriend's booth, and he was not there! I looked for him, but could not find him. Does this mean that I

have a grudge against my boyfriend or he has done me wrong?

–Worried

Dear Worried,

Don't worry, be happy! And for heaven's sake, forgive yourself and all of those people from your past who are still weighing on your mind after all this time. A big clearing is in order. Just think of all those people, write one big letter expressing how you feel and then burn it. Let all those bad feelings go. You will feel so much lighter; you will feel more free and be more accepting of yourself. As far as your boyfriend goes, it is time to be honest with yourself. In a nutshell, it was you who walked away from him first, and for the purpose of checking out other action. You then got upset with him because he did not stay in one place and wait for you. This is an outside point of view and may not be valid, however, it is something to take a closer look at. My take is that you are harboring a lot of resentment from the pain of your past, while also projecting onto your boyfriend your doubts and suspicions resulting from that. This, paired with the fact that you are still looking at other options, would suggest that you are not entirely sure about or "sold" on this relationship for whatever reason. I would examine your own motives and agendas, looking into your own heart to see what is really going on there. Your dream painted a very clear picture, now it is up to you to decide if this is the right relationship for you or not.

Dear Laura,

I had a dream that I was with my new man and his 4-year-old daughter, Rachel. We were out walking, and we came upon a patch of dirt, you know, the kind with ooze and silt. Rachel was dying to go in it. Her dad kept telling her no and I said "Gee, Dad, you are no fun," and took off my shoes and walked in it. Rachel (already barefoot) joined me and we had a wonderful time walking around in the ooze, slipping and sliding all over the place. The more Dad protested, the more we laughed and the dirtier we got! Finally, Dad gave up and joined us and we all got very muddy. What does this say, if anything, about our new relationship?

–Muddy in Mississippi

Dear Muddy,

What a great dream! I would say that this is a very healthy relationship that you are in, as your are confident with yourself and comfortable enough with your new man and his daughter to really let loose and enjoy yourself. Walking barefoot and stepping in the ooze and silt shows that you are connecting with the earth and to your spirit, baring your soul as you bare your "soles," so to speak. Life truly does imitate art with this dream, as the daughter so accurately depicts your inner child with whom you are thrilled to be connecting with, and the father aka your boyfriend, represents your inner authority figure, which you take great pleasure in defying, thus granting yourself permission to have fun. The fact that your man puts up a fight and then gives in and joins you and his daughter shows that he knows how to be the responsible adult and good parental role model, yet is not so stern that he cannot relax and enjoy himself, too, which he ultimately does. This dream is about balance... adult and child, male and female. I am sensing that you are embarking on a great adventure with these two, and that this one is a keeper, according to your subconscious.

I am certain that after reading both of these wonderful nocturnal entries submitted by my readers that you can see the difference between a dream of affirmation and a cautionary tale. Not all dreams will be this obvious, so it is up to you, the dreamer, to take the time to break it down and crack your own dream code. We will talk more about this in Chapter Eight, however, I am confident that you can do this. It is like a muscle, the more you work it, the stronger it gets.

Chapter Six: Fantasies and Desires in Dreams and What Secrets They Reveal

To dream is to escape our sometimes mundane reality. Some dreams happen with our eyes open and those are called daydreams. Remember little Ralphie from "Christmas Story" who was daydreaming about his Red Rider BB gun? He was so immersed in the daydream that his teacher had to snap him out of his reverie by waving her hand in front of his face. How many times have you been at work and envisioning yourself on a tropical beach somewhere? To have a daydream is to transport yourself to another time and place; past, present or future. You are utilizing your powers of visualization to take yourself out of your current situation and into something more desirable, even if it is only for a moment. Your daydreams are always about something pleasurable… no one drifts off and sees demons or devils, for example. It is usually something you want, like winning the lottery, going on an amazing vacation or a date with that handsome stranger. You can picture it so clearly that is seems real. You are awake when this happens, and this is a way of getting in touch with your conscious desires and giving yourself a pleasant midday break.

What about the other dreams we have while we are sleeping that take us places we normally would not go? What do those mean? Our subconscious mind, the ultimate detective, is aware of everything: The time on the clock, the temperature in the room, the feeling of the watch or jewelry one wears, the background noises, etc. It observes and records everything that we experience in our lives from the moment of conception. It will make note of the handsome stranger you see on the street, the sexy models in the magazines you read, the erotic scenes in the shows or movies that you watch… all of this and more is stored in the vast warehouse of your subconscious mind.

The thoughts that you think and the feelings that you have are all a part of this, too. For example, the attractive co-worker you notice each day at work, the actor you have a crush on, the musician you fancy – all of this is noted on the log sheet before it is stored in the warehouse. So when you go to sleep and experience a myriad of sexual images, this does not mean that you are a freak (well, maybe just a wee bit). It means that what you witness, observe and experience during the day will play out at night in your dreams.

A common scenario is to dream of being naked in public. To have this dream would suggest, for some, that you are either feeling vulnerable and exposed, or acting on the desire to "let it all hang out." This would depend on your nature, of course. Are you the closeted type or an extreme exhibitionist? If you are actively living the nudist lifestyle, for example, this dream would not have the same meaning for you as it would for someone who is more conservative about nudity.

Other common scenarios might include dreaming of being raped. I am not talking brutal gang rape in "The Accused" movie or "Straw Dogs" style. Being raped by someone you desire is a common fantasy for women, as they are giving in to carnal desires and most always it involves someone they have an attraction toward. Something that maybe you would never do, but in your dream you do not have to take any responsibility as this handsome stranger overtakes you and you are powerless. It can also be a popular dream for someone who is always in control to give up control. I was told by a dominatrix that her clientele are mostly CEOs of companies and people with high-powered jobs who seek her services. These men are so dominant at work that, of course, their fantasy outside of work is to be dominated.

Other common scenarios are dreaming of having sex with inappropriate partners or engaging in deviant sexual behaviors. Note that the words inappropriate and deviant are subject to interpretation, as what is deemed freaky to one person is run-of-the-mill for another. If your sexual style is more of the vanilla variety, and you dream that you are acting out a scene from "50 Shades of Grey" with your son's hot soccer coach or the mouthwatering personal trainer from the gym, then you are probably yearning to broaden your sexual horizons a bit. Conversely, if you dream that your priest (sacred) and funeral home director (morbid) are engaging in acts that you find distasteful or unpleasant, then this is probably not a dream about hidden desires, but more about integrating aspects of the self as a whole.

Yet another very common scenario is that you are married or committed, yet you find yourself attracted to someone other than your mate. If your morals prevent you from acting on that impulse, which would be the case for a lot of people, then you may find yourself engaging in a daydream… or a sexual fantasy where you imagine what it might be like to touch, taste and feel the object of your desire. If you do not act on them, these desires may come out even stronger in your nocturnal state: They may be very vivid and graphic, going to the places where your conscious mind would never dare to venture. It is as if you get to sample the goods without suffering the consequences when you have dream sex. This is also a good barometer of your limits and boundaries and can serve as a moral compass. How did you feel upon waking? Were you exhilarated or guilt ridden? It is important to pay attention to the feeling in the dream and notice if it changes after you wake up or throughout the day.

Regardless of what you may be feeling, having these dream experiences affords you the opportunity for increased self-discovery in a safe environment (your bedroom) and to choose what to discard and what to keep as your reality. You can explore your inner self and indulge in your wildest fantasies without ever hurting anyone. Conversely, you can use your dreaming mind to go a step further with lucid dreaming, where you can be an active participant rather than a passive observer… "A little more to the left… oh yeah, that's the spot." Lucid dreaming is another subject entirely, and many books have been written on the subject, if that is something you are interest in exploring further.

If you do find yourself dreaming of sex often, it could mean that you are repressing your physical needs and require an outlet, or if you have a healthy sex life, it may simply be an expression of that. I find that when I am in a good relationship,

I tend to replay the encounters in my dreams, which is oh-so-nice! Ahhh.

Dreaming of a rock star, actor or model you will likely never meet face-to-face is a fantasy dream… and aren't those always the best? I think we all wake up from that type of dream and no further analysis is required. It is more like "I dreamt that I had sex with so and so. It was awesome! The end." It may seem obvious when it is someone that you have a monster crush on that it is just about the sex, however, do yourself a favor and dig a little deeper. "Who wouldn't want to have sex with Brad Pitt?" you say. Well, quite a few people, Angelina Jolie included, absolutely would. That is too easy. Ask yourself "Who is Brad Pitt and why do I like him?" (Angelina if you are a man). If I had a dream about Brad Pitt, my analysis would go something like this:

Brad Pitt: Handsome actor, devoted husband and father, humanitarian. I would add that he hails from a small town, appears to be somewhat humble, also very intelligent and articulate. By taking all of these elements and putting them together, you will see that not only are you hankering for a piece of him physically, he also has qualities that you would like to possess or expand on. If you are a heterosexual man and you dream of Brad Pitt, it does not have to mean that you desire him sexually; it possibly means that he is a cool guy whom you admire and that you would like to be more like him. The same would ring true for the straight woman who dreams of Angelina, although her extraordinary beauty might be cause for some to reconsider.

What if you dream of being with sexual with someone you despise? Does that mean that you have a poor self-image or that you secretly desire that person? I would suggest looking more closely at this person and repeating the same steps that you would do for the Brad or Angelina dream. What role does this person play in your life? What are some of the good qualities that you have in common with this person? Conversely, what are some of the less positive traits that you share? You may think that there is no way that you could possibly have even one iota of common ground with someone that you harbor such ill will, however, I am telling you that you most certainly do. That person appeared in you dream because your subconscious mind wants to show you something. What is it about this person that you do not like and what does that say about you? Is this man or woman rude, for example? Arrogant? Whatever you find, there is a message for you there. It does not mean that you desire this person, unless of course, you really do. In most cases, dreaming of being sexual with some you dislike is an opportunity to work on accepting the aspects of yourself that you are not comfortable with and do not acknowledge, in the privacy of your own bedroom.

Here is an example of a dream from one of my readers that illustrates this.

Dear Laura,

What does it mean to dream of a prostitute? Last night I had a dream that I was at a party where there were Asian prostitutes, and I was trying to turn the volume down on the TV and radio. A lot of

my friends were there. Does this have any significance?

–D.C.

Dear D.C.,

Anything that shows up in a dream has significance. There is always a meaning or a lesson to learn. Are you Asian? I ask to determine why the Asian women are featured in your dream, as there are prostitutes of every race. Asian women are stereotyped as being very subservient. To dream of a prostitute can mean that you are either selling yourself short in some way or that you are being seduced by something that does not serve your best interests or highest good. I am sensing that maybe you are in a relationship where your needs are not being met and the Asian prostitutes (subservient women selling themselves) are a mirror of you settling for less than you know you deserve. If this pertains to your sex life directly, then perhaps it is time to speak up and ask for what you want, in and out of bed!

As for reducing the volume on the TV and radio, it would appear as if there are too many distractions in your life at this time, that you are drowning out the "inner voice" that we all have. This is a reminder for you to tune into your higher self. This may also refer to control issues, as well. Remember, you always have the right to choose what you watch and listen to. I would look at your wants/needs sexually and romantically, and see how this applies.

Chapter Seven: Write Your Own Dream Story: The Role of Your Dream Journal

The act of keeping a dream journal is vital to your dreaming life. It is very simple and easy to do. If you are not in the habit of journaling, then it may seem daunting, however, it is really just the opposite. All you have to do is get a notebook, or you can even create an online journal, if that is your preference. I love writing my dreams down with a ball point pen in a nice colorful journal, but that is simply my preference… you must do what feels most comfortable for you. You can have a very basic looking journal or make it fancy. I believe you can find dedicated dream journals in New Age bookstores. Whatever you choose to use to record your dreams is not as important as the act of recording them. If you are pressed for time in the morning, you can send yourself a voice message and then record it later. Whatever works for you, so long as you get it done. Not recording your dreams is like not reading an urgent telegram. There are important messages for you in each and every dream.

The first thing to do is to make note of the date and give your dream a title so that you can reference it easily. "June 23, Handsome Stranger in Elevator" is an example of how you can easily recall and reference a dream. Write the dream down as if you were telling it to someone else. Remember the story and anything unusual that stands out.

Were there vivid colors? Who were the people involved? What was your role? Were you a participant or an observer? How did you feel during the dream and was it the same feeling that you had upon awakening? Did the feeling change after some time had passed?

If you dreamed about a handsome actor, for example, that would probably give you a good feeling during and afterward and would not be likely to change. Conversely, to dream of having sex with a sibling might give you an "ick" feeling initially, but after further exploration, you might see that the dream was not about sex but about cultivating the qualities you admire in your sibling.

Take note of every single detail that you can recall about the dream. Go back to it later if you have any further insight or awareness. The more you do this, the more you will get into the habit of doing this, and your dream recall will improve greatly, as you are conditioning your mind to remember.

Chapter Eight: Dream Journal Exercises

Here is an example of how to quickly and easily break your dream apart, identify the symbols, and then put it all back together, using a dream from one of my readers.

Dear Laura,

I really need your help with this one. First, let me supply you with some background information. Vic is an old friend with whom I have starred in show biz. I am working on a television show with him currently. David is my brother. I have not spoken to him in years, his choice. The relatives were executors in my aunt's estate, who we suspect cheated us on our inheritances. I have just become involved with someone who is planning to move to L.A. in July. Here goes: *I am in my relative's apartment. They are out of town. I see Vic talking to a woman. I get the impression that she is a prostitute and Vic is enlisting her services for me. I tell Vic to forget it! I am outside now, loading my belongings onto a trailer. The woman is standing beside me, giving me advice about reputable movers. I tell her I have been burned by reputable movers. She leaves. I am back in the apartment now, and the woman is half-undressed on the sofa with my brother David. It is apparent that her seduction of him was a failure. I go into the bedroom and lie down. She enters and begins to seduce me, and I become a willing participant! Just then, a large black and white cat jumps on the bed. I shoo the cat away, and suddenly the room is full of kittens. The woman begins to gently pick them up and remove them. I again lose interest in the woman and leave. I run into Vic in the hall, who tells me to hurry up because* he *knows that my relative will soon be returning. I would appreciate any insights you may have on this.*

–Bert

Dear Bert,

It sounds as if you are having doubts about your new relationship, however, I feel that it has more to do with you than with her. Your female side must be embraced, and when it is, you will be able to relate better to the opposite sex. You yearn to be more creative, yet your practical side dominates. Do you see my point? Accept this part of yourself and express it. This is the essence of your dream. The kittens portray your budding female energy in a very non-threatening manner, yet you are quick to push them aside. Play with them if they come to see you again. They are black and white, which represents the yin and the yang, duality, etc. To see a prostitute in your dream suggests that you may be selling yourself short or that you are being seduced by something that is not what you want to be involved in. I would be wary of the people you surround yourself with, as your dream suggests people of ill intent are all around you.

That was my interpretation or take on Bert's dream. Let's pretend for a moment that this is your dream and break it down into bite sized pieces using the symbols. I am using a literal

49

definition for each, but is up to you to add your own meaning to each one so that the interpretation will truly be your own.

Prostitutes: Women who walk the streets and trade sex for money
Kittens: Baby cats
Black: A color
White: A color
Vic: Old friend
David: Brother with whom you are somewhat estranged
Movers: People who transport furniture from one place to the next
Apartment: Smaller space to live, often temporary
Relatives: Those related to you
Sofa: A piece of furniture intended for relaxation, socializing or watching TV. Some people sleep on a sofa.

What I would like for you to do now is to take each symbol, give it your own meaning and put it back together. Act as if this were your dream and rely only on your own symbols rather than those of someone else.

If you repeat these steps with each and every dream that you have, you will be able to interpret all of your own dreams, all of the time, without relying on anything or anyone. Just yourself.

Chapter Nine: Preparing Yourself for the Perfect Night of Dreaming: Manifesting Your Dream Lover

If your wish is to have dreams of love and romance, what should you do to start preparing yourself for the perfect night of dreaming? I suggest you start by having a delicious meal, something that you truly enjoy paired with a nice glass of wine or champagne. And, of course, a succulent dessert would be included in this decadent meal. Set the mood by having soft music playing in the background and perhaps lighting a candle. Fresh flowers to accent the table is a nice touch. After you have enjoyed your meal, draw a warm bath for yourself. Add some aromatherapy bath salts into the water or add bubbles, whichever you prefer. Sipping champagne while taking a warm bubble bath is a great way to relax and unwind from the day's events. Just let everything go and think about the nice meal you just enjoyed. Think of how soothing the warm water feels and how smooth the champagne or wine you are drinking tastes. Notice how your body is starting to relax, muscle by muscle, from the top of your head to the tips of your toes. Just allow the warm water to engulf you. Let your mind go… let it wander… brush away thought of bills, laundry, etc. and let it go someplace faraway. Maybe you will travel to a foreign land. Maybe you will be on a tropical beach. Just let your mind go wherever it chooses to go.

After you exit the bath, apply some good quality lotion to your skin. It does not have to be expensive, but it should feel expensive. Let it soak in. Notice how your body responds to all the loving attention you are lavishing on it. Once the lotion is absorbed by your skin, put on your favorite pajamas… or if you prefer to sleep in the buff… by all means, do that. Make sure there are clean sheets on the bed. Spritz aromatherapy, perfume or cologne on your pillow… a scent that you find sexy and appealing. Take out a piece of paper and write "Tonight I will dream of love and romance." Put it near where you sleep. Listen to music that you feel is conducive to love and romance. Something sultry, of course. Make sure that the temperature in your bedroom is to your liking, neither too warm nor too cool, and that there are no distractions. Doors locked, lights out, etc. Slide into your comfortable bed and take notice of the scents and sounds, as you drift into a peaceful slumber.

As you are drifting off to sleep, think about your dream lover. What does he or she look like? What kind of energy does he or she emit? What is the feeling that you get when you connect with this lover? What does your lover's touch feel like? What is the first kiss like with your lover? Let your mind wander as you embark on the delicious voyage, feeling yourself melting like a warm pool of butter as you savor this experience.

You will want to record every detail that you can recall upon awakening. You may be surprised by what you find.

Your lover may be different that what you originally anticipated, however, be open to it. You may be pleasantly surprised if the reality surpasses the fantasy when you meet this lover in the flesh.

Conclusion

I hope that you have enjoyed going on this journey with me and that you will take the time to record your dreams, interpret them, and fully understand the message that each contains.

I invite you to look at my dream dictionary on my website (www.inyourdreambooks.com) of possible meanings or any dream dictionary if you get stuck or want some food for thought. However, it is always best to ask yourself not what a symbol means but what it means to you. If you do this habitually, I know that not one dream will come to you that you cannot eventually understand the true meaning of after a period of reflection.

I will say that it does take time and practice, and that is where your dream journal comes in handy to assist you. If you get into the habit of recording your dreams daily, or however often you recall them, you will be able to spot patterns or themes.

If it is a recurrent dream that you are having, it is something that you are ignoring that needs to be resolved within yourself. You will likely keep having this dream until you address it. Sometimes a dream will come, and the meaning will not be clear for several weeks or months. Be patient because you will eventually get that clarity, especially when it is a precognitive dream – those are dreams of future events and may take a while to manifest into the physical realm.

I have a gift for you, an online journal that you can use to record your dreams, available at inyourdreambooks.com. I also have two more books coming up in the series that I encourage you to read. One is "Your Dreams of Luck, Money and Success and What They Mean" and the other is "Welcome to Your Nightmares: Monsters, Demons and Just Plain Scary Dreams," which will be both be published this year.

Please like and share my Facebook page "In Your Dreams by Laura Suzanne." You can also email me at info@inyourdreamsbooks.com if you would like help with interpreting your dream. I will walk you through the steps and guide you on your way to gaining better understanding and clarity with your dreams. Visit my website for additional information about my services at www.inyourdreambooks.com.

Author Bio

Laura Suzanne Snell was born and raised in the San Francisco Bay Area and now resides in Las Vegas, with her beloved cat, Tiger. Laura is a graduate of San Diego State University where she received a Bachelor of Science degree in Psychology. A lifelong student of parapsychology and metaphysical enthusiast, Laura has read many books on the subject of dreams and further expanded her knowledge by taking additional courses through the Dream Interpretation Institute and by becoming a Certified Dream Guide. Curious to learn even more about the inner workings of the subconscious mind, Ms. Snell enrolled in courses at Serenus Clinical Hypnosis and added Certified Clinical Hypnotherapist to her resume. After having a profound experience with energetic healing that instantly cured her of a long-standing medical condition, she became a Certified Usui Reiki Master Practitioner/Teacher initiated by Susan Fox of Virginia.

Laura has written articles for Las Vegas Image Magazine and had a column featuring dream interpretation called "In Your Dreams" in Las Vegas Weekly. She has been a frequent guest on local radio stations, including KLAV and 97.1 The Point, in addition to co-hosting a radio show with Master Hypnotherapist Victoria Gallagher called"Hyptalk," where holistic health and metaphysics were the focus. She has taught classes and hosted workshops at bookstores and health food stores, such as Borders and Whole Foods in Las Vegas.

Laura is highly intuitive and empathic, making her a natural for assisting others in discovering the deeper meanings of even the most bizarre or complex dreams. Let her be your guide to solving the mystery of your dreams by reading her book series and following the do it yourself instructions, tips and suggestions she has provided for you. You will find that with a little effort you will soon become a pro at decoding your own dreams and that is her wish for you.

9 781943 843152